GW00384522

"If Memory be Truth..."

Poems
Hymns
Meditative Verse
with Notes

Stanley Hemming-Clark

© Searchline Publishing 2017
First printed 2017

ISBN: 978 1 897864 33 3

Published by Searchline Publishing
Searchline House, Holbrook Lane, Chislehurst, BR7 6PE, UK
Tel & Fax: +44 (0)20 8295 0739
www.inyougo.webeden.co.uk

All rights reserved

No part of this publication may be reproduced, or stored in a
retrieval system, or transmitted, in any form or by any means,
mechanical, electronic, photocopying, recording or otherwise,
without the permission of Searchline Publishing.

Printed by http://www.catfordprint.co.uk/

About the author
The author read Latin and French and Theology at Cambridge.
He was ordained in the Church of England in 1955. For 38 years
he was vicar of a village church in Kent, combining this with the
chaplaincy of a convalescent home and later teaching Religious
Education, Latin and Classical Civilisation. He now lives near
Guildford, officiates as needed in Surrey churches, and teaches
Latin to a U3A group.

Front cover: Surrey Hills

Introduction by the author

This book contains poems, hymns, meditative verse and notes, written over a period of several years. It takes its title from the first poem, "If Memory be Truth..." When I put these verses together, this emerged as a theme to give a pattern to the book. This is the thought of memory keeping the past alive in a changing world and in personal growth. This theme, which is the basis of the opening verses, recurs several times throughout the book, and is taken up more fully in the closing verses. Here the person of Christ is shown to gather up past, present and future.: Memory is given a specifically Christian sense in the Holy Eucharist, which itself is a focal point in the life of union with Christ. So having begun with human experiences of change and loss, we finish with a deeper experience of fulfilment.

Other verses and meditations deal with a number of themes including bereavement and questionings. A few hymns have been sung in our village churches: some meditations used at a Christian support ministry or in sermons. Their form is traditionally structured, including some sonnets, even where deep personal feeling is involved.

If Memory Be Truth. A Sonnet

I longed to see it once again – that scene
Of long-lost youth: new birth of life each spring,
Leaves laughing in a thousand shades of green,
Green hedges where a hundred birds could sing:
Cool paths through woods or by a lonely field,
And fish rejoicing in clear-watered stream;
Deep darkness by the night-time skies revealed:
Through passing years remembered in a dream.
    At last I come: in grey old age return.
    No hedges left: not birds' but traffic's sound:
    Hard concrete road, where night-time headlights burn:
    The stream polluted where no fish are found.
    All things are changed – myself – the scenes of youth –
    Yet all remain, if memory be truth.

This poem was first published in the Christmas 1998 issue of *The Countryman* magazine. It can be read on two levels. Firstly, it is obviously a piece of nostalgia, expressing grief at the loss of the natural and rural world through urbanisation. Secondly, it raises the philosophical questions of whether this vanished world still exists and if so, how? The concluding thought is that it remains within our memory and therefore as part of us.

In the well-known passage at the beginning of A la Recherche du Temps Perdu, Proust described how as he drank tea, he was reminded of how his aunt used to give him a Madeleine dipped in tea – "Et tout d'un coup le souvenir m'est apparu..." All his early life came back into his mind. At the end, after the thought of the past brought into the present by images, encapsulated in a work of art, he wrote, "J'éprouvais un sentiment de fatigue et d'effroi à sentir que tout ce temps si long non seulement avait, sans une interruption, été vécu, pensée, sécreté par moi, mais qu'il était ma vie..."

"Nun Wer... ist ein Mensch" A Sonnet

I do not envy those who've just begun
Their lives, though youth and strength and hopes they hold –
The carefree child, whose day ahead looks fun,
The boys and girls with forward glance grown bold,
Lovers rejoicing in their private dawn,
Career-beginners whose success is willed.
These are not theirs – those years as yet unborn:
They are but dreams which may not be fulfilled.
I have been once, and in a sense remain,
A child at heart with wonder at the world,
An eager lover knowing joy and pain,
Husband and father, with career unfurled.
My past years all exist and in my heart
Growing fulfilment to advancing years impart.

This poem was partly inspired by a passage written by Kästner
(1899-1974), whose best-known work in England is probably
Emil and the Detectives. The passage here referred to comes
from Ansprache zum Schulbeginn. "Lasst euch die Kindheit nicht
austreiben! Schaut, die meisten Menschen legen ihre Kindheit ab
wie einen alten Hut... Früher waren sie Kinder, dann wurden sie
Erwachsene, aber was sind sie nun? Nur wer erwachsen wird und
Kind bleibt, ist ein Mensch!" (Do not let your childhood be cast
out! Most people lay aside their childhood like an old hat...
Earlier they were children, then they became adults, but what are
they now? Only the one who has grown up and remains a child is
a Person.) Kästner gives other examples – an out-of-date
telephone number, a sausage which is eaten and no longer exists.
The stages of life are not like these. Because they become part of
us, they still exist.

This poem develops this thought, originally written by Kästner
for children. It adds the thought, from the perspective of old age,
that we need not envy those who are younger.

First Love. A Sonnet

There was soft magic in the woods that night:
They were so young: young seemed the world around.
When first they kissed and held each other tight,
First words of love then deafened other sound.
To hear each other's speech had been such fun
(How sweet new words in accent strange can seem!)
And then they felt their lives had just begun,
Made plans together with a youthful dream.
She left: no more they met: their letters told
Of happy marriages, of work and play...
Children, grandchildren...and then themselves grown old.
At last a printed card – her Funeral Day.
He wondered – "Through long years, had I some part,
As she in mine, in a still youthful heart?"

This poem expresses something of the poignancy and special character of fist love. In style there is a deliberate contrast between the dreamy, romantic tone of the first part and the brisk, factual tone of the second. It contains the thought that however happy a marriage and family is, an early love has not simply passed into non-existence, it remains in our memory, but in a deeper sense than "non-forgetfulness." It has become part of us, taking up the thought of the first two poems.

The thought of "magic" in line 1 is taken up in the poem Transfiguration (pages 18 and 19). There magic transformation is shown in a deeper and fuller sense – but not disparate, since human loves are an image of God's love (pages 14 and 15).

Three Sonnets For Stella

The next three poems were written for my wife Stella who passed from this life in 2010 after fifty-five years of a happy marriage. Thoughts and emotions are expressed in traditionally structured poems. Although they are deeply personal, they are included here in the hope that they may help others facing a similar loss. Each ones begins with the kind of questioning that we all have, but ends in a note of confident certainty, based on revelation.

The Christian hope is ultimately based on, "the glorious appearing of our Lord Jesus Christ" (Titus 2:13). Much is uncertain and beyond imagination in the present life of the departed. Two essential points which are certain were well expressed in a 1979 Letter for the Congregation for the Doctrine of the Faith.

The first is the continuity with our present life in Christ.

The second is a radical difference, for to be "with Christ" contains a promise pointing to a wonderful mystery. "It does not yet appear what we shall be, but we know that when he appears we shall be like him, for we shall see him as he is" (1 John 3:2).

Since these two points are based on revelation in Sacred Scripture, they offer a firm consolations to the bereaved. The future life is a "mystery" not because it is uncertain, but because it is more wonderful than can be imagined or expressed.

That is why each of these three poems after questionings ends on a note of confidence.

How Shall I See You?

How shall I see you when we meet once more?
Against a dying light you did not rage,
But gentle smiled at light from further shore.
Transformed in light, how will appear your age?
With youth restored, as on our wedding day?
Or thirty-three, the year our Lord arose?
Or as at last farewell with hair turned grey?
Wond'ring we ask of what no mortal knows.
One thing we know, that we will shed no tear
When I in turn put off this form grown old,
Or when Our Lord in glory shall appear
His form to share, whose face we shall behold.
      Transformed, yet still the one we knew before,
      So shall I see you when we meet once more.

Passages from Holy Scripture
Luke 24: 13-27; Mark 16: 12
Matthew 22: 23-33; Mark 12: 18-27; Luke 20: 27-40
Matthew 17: 1-8; Mark 9: 2-8; Luke 9: 28-36
1 Corinthians 15; 2 Corinthians 5: 1-5; Philippians 3: 21
1 John 3: 1-3; Isaiah 40: 29-31

This poem and notes were first read at the Loseley Christian
Parkinson Help Centre, where some have been bereaved. The
reference to thirty-three years in line 6 is explained on the facing
page. Thoughts along these lines may help those whose child has
died in infancy, or who face any form of suffering. They may have
some bearing on the fact that different people have known the
departed at different stages of their earthly life. For the last two
lines see Transfiguration on page 18.

How Shall I See You? Notes
Lines 2 and 3
A reference to the well-known poem by Dylan Thomas
> Do not go gentle into that good night,
> Old age should burn and rave at close of day:
> Rage, rage against the dying of the light.

Line 6
The belief that the resurrection bodies of the redeemed are perfect and not subject to the limitations of the earthly bodies has dogmatic authority, being based on revelation in Holy Scriptures. Some theologians have expressed this as being the age of about thirty-three – the age at which our Lord arose and the age of perfect development.

St Augustine
AS for St Paul's words of the measure of the fullness of Christ, they either imply that all his members as then being joined with Him in the Head, should make up the time's consummation, or if they tend to the resurrection, the meaning is that all should arise neither younger nor older. But just of the age at which Christ Himself suffered and rose again. For the learned authors of this world say that about thirty years man is in his full state, and from that age he declines to an age of more gravity and decay.

City of God: Book 22: Chapter 15

St Thomas Aquinas
(Quoting Ephesians 4: 13) Christ rose in the state of youth (in aetate iuvenili) which begins at about thirty years, as Augustine says. Therefore others too rise in the state of youth.

Man will rise again without any defect of human nature, because just as God founded human nature without defect, thus He will restore it without defect. Now human nature is deficient in two ways: in one way because it has not yet reached its final perfection, and in a second way because it has already receded from its ultimate perfection.

In the first way it is deficient in children: in the second way in the aged. So in each of these human nature will be brought back by the resurrection to the state of final perfection, which is in the state of youth (in aetate iuvenili), towards which the movement of growth is terminated and from which the movement of degeneration begins.
Supp. 3: 81: 1

Do You Imagine?

Do you imagine now the place we met?
And is the time within your memory still?
Or in th'eternal world do you forget
The place and time beside a Surrey hill?
Sometimes I pass the place which looks the same:
The time seems yesterday or long ago.
I see your photo, speak aloud your name,
And wonder. Can you hear or do you know?
Can you recall the days we used to share
When in our life and work you played a part?
Can you uphold my work with heavenly prayer
Whose source is knowledge or a loving heart?
       But I know you rest, awake or sleeping.
       Til next we meet, safe in God's keeping.

This poem speaks of the memory of love and past experience,
made vivid by familiar scenes. With these thoughts we ponder
the question about those whom we love but do not see – how
much do they remember of the past, know and help in our
present life? With regard to "help", the words of Ste Thérèse of
Licieux come to mind: "Si le bon Dieu exauce mes désires, mon
ciel se passera sur la terre jusqu'à la fin du monde. Oui, je veux
passer mon Ciel à faire du bien sur la terre."

The poem finishes on a note of confident certainty.

8

Was It A Dream?

Was it a dream last night? Or did we share
Some time together? It was like a dream
With time and place confused. Yet you were there,
Our lives the same as they had always been.
We spoke as in the old familiar way
And laughed together as in days long gone.
The dream then vanished with the light of day
And you were gone and I was left alone.
Perhaps between my world of time and space
And your eternal world the veil is slight.....?
So had I pierced that veil to see your face.....?
Or had you come to me in still of night.....?
More than dreams I know we're closest where
Earth and heaven their threefold Sanctus share.

Probably we all dream of those whom we love and who are no longer
with us. Sometimes the ages, setting and events are confused, even if
vivid. This poem questions in a perhaps imaginative way whether there
has been a real encounter.
The sudden confident ending to these questionings assures us that it is
in the act of worship, as a real encounter with God, that we come closest
to those whom we love. This is especially true of the Holy Eucharist,
focussed here on the Sanctus. This is the song of the heavenly choir
(Isaiah 6:3 and Apocalypse 4:8). The church on earth joins in this
worship, expressed in the Liturgy. The words express a reality which the
Orthodox Church stresses as the heart of worship. We think of the well-
known story of Vladimir, Prince of Kiev, still a pagan, coming to
Constantinople. After attending Orthodox worship, he commented –
"We did not know whether we were in heaven or on earth." Here we
embrace two worlds at once. Here above all, not in vague dreams or
wistful imaginings, should we be aware of those whom we love. A recent
survey suggested that many people who are uncertain about God,
believe in a future life with those whom we love. For the Christian, this
reverses the order. The "share" of verse one is echoed by the "share" in
verse 14. The personal sharing in dream is less than the church's
worship sharing the angelic song of Holy, Holy, Holy.

Imperfect now, our worship looks onward to its fulfilment in the new
creation, which some other poems express.

Four Sonnets of Peace and War

The Unmarried

They smiled at her, those girls of youthful charms,
Puzzled, amused, a few with gentle scorn,
Secure, possessive on their boyfriends' arms,
They thought at eighty-three she looked forlorn.
As long as people knew, she'd looked the same –
With small black dog of never changing breed:
When one dog died, the next one took his name.
They thought, though strange, this met some inner need.
Once she had loved like them (How could they know?),
Had dreams of marriage, home, and children shared.
His gift a small black dog (so long ago)
Before he went to war and was not spared.
　　　With boyfriend's gift, though sixty years had passed,
　　　Twenty at heart, she knew her love would last.

This poem expresses the sadness and waste of war. It is based
upon a real person, now departed, whose life was known only to
a few. The opening lines imagine how others saw her. Unlike the
one in the poem "First Love", she had never known marriage and
children. As described in the extract from Kästner, the past was
still with her, even in outward actions, all through her life.

The Widow

All stopped and gathered round to hear their guide,
All chatting ceased, all listened to his words –
Descriptions, well-worn jokes upon the side –
"That island there – a special haunt of birds".
"Saint Paul once sailed across this very sea".
"That cove – old Greeks in legend told its fame".
"A British ship was sunk in forty three". –
They licked their ices as he told its name...
Old history now: chatting, they moved away.
Heedless of these, her thoughts kept one behind,
Thoughts of lost youth, of hopes one long-gone day,
Thoughts of one sailor living in her mind...
      Still, silent, she gazed: that now peaceful wave
      Had hid for fifty years her husband's grave.

In its particular presentation, this poem is imaginative. The idea came during a boat trip off the island of Malta. There are, however, many who lie buried at sea, whose ships are their final resting places.

Multiply these two poems by several millions and we sense the waste, suffering and futility of war.

We also see the contrast between the outward gaiety of some and the loss borne by others. In a wider sense we see how people may appear to others who do not know their experiences and thoughts.

The Classics Professor

Ten years of work were now at last complete.
At peace himself and with the world he knew.
In comfy chair relaxed, stretched out his feet,
Glass by his side, on his old pipe he drew.
Ten years upon that Latin text he'd spent:
He could its varied manuscripts compare.
Show what the poet's subtle mind had meant.
Explain each point of grammar with due care.
Slowly he read his preface through once more.
"Some fine young men," he thought, "will read my book,"
Added the date, "July – one – nine – one – four,"
Then gave The Times a quick and casual look –
"Balkans... not our concern... some Archduke dead."
Put out the lamp and went in peace to bed.

This poem was written after reading a Roman author, one of
those editions where the notes are longer than the text itself.
Then I saw the date of the preface – May 1914. I imagined the
author writing it after years of study and research, feeling secure
in a world that was soon to be overwhelmed by catastrophe.

Many of the "fine young men" whom he visualised studying his
book as undergraduates would soon lie dead on the Western
Front. The final line suggests the well-known words of Grey in
August 1914, "The lamps are going out all over Europe: we shall
not see them lit again in our lifetime".

The Chairman of the Arms Manufacturing Company

The Arms Company Chairman spoke with delight,
The Shareholders rubbed their hands with great glee,
The Bankers approved the deal as just right,
The Government praised the increased GNP.
Several million pounds, said the Sales Contract,
Fighter planes and arms to a foreign land
Where (don't mention this embarrassing fact)
Most human rights and the Church were all banned.
When challenged they could their excuses all plead –
"Ten thousand jobs, without this we'll all fail."
"Those who buy them are an ally we need."
"Others will make, if we don't, this great sale".
The Chairman in church thought of men who had died,
"Give peace in our time, O Lord," he then cried.

This poem was written after reading of the possible cancellation
of a very large contract for selling arms to a country whose
human rights record had been criticised. It expresses the fact that
we as a nation manufacture and sell arms, but also remember the
fallen and pray for peace, especially on Remembrance Sunday. It
refers to the number of jobs which depend on this. Similar
examples come to mind – those whose jobs depended on driving
trains to Auschwitz or involvement in the slave trade, which
recent programmes show to have involved a surprisingly large
number of people. The poem therefore rather than simply
denouncing hypocrisy, suggests a moral dilemma.

Hymn   **Tune: Abbot's Leigh**

God is love, is love supernal
Ere the worlds began to be,
Uncreated love eternal,
God, one God in Persons three.
Far beyond our mind or sighting
Lies God's Being innermost,
Persons three with love uniting
Father, Son and Holy Ghost.

God is love, his love o'erflowing
Gave our lovely world its birth,
Heaven's gift of love bestowing
To created life on earth.
God in love ordained that wearing
Image of himself as sign,
Human earthly loves are sharing
Heaven's life of love divine.

God is love, he has declared it
When the Son as man was seen.
In the Word made flesh he shared it,
Fallen nature to redeem.
He for love of us descended
In atonement for our wrong,
His the love, not ours, proclaimèd
Now and ever in our song.

God is love, shown in the sending
Of the Spirit through the Son,
By whose life in love unending
All his people may be one.
For we know within us dwelling
Spirit whom the Father gave,
Testifying and forthtelling
Jesus came to the world to save.

God is love: his love supernal,
Long from earthly minds concealed,
Draws us to the life eternal,
Son and Spirit have revealed.
In that love enfolded, living,
Trusting where we cannot see,
Praise we offer and thanksgiving
To the Blessèd Trinity.

14

The Holy Trinity and God Is Love

The hymn on the facing page was first sung on Trinity Sunday 2015, the 60th anniversary of the author's ordination to the priesthood.

The main passage of Holy Scripture on which this is based is 1 John 4: 7-16.

The church has always taught that, while the existence of God may be inferred from the created world (e.g. Romans 1: 19-20), the very nature of God as Holy Trinity is a matter of revelation, revealed in the sending of the Son and the Spirit. "God himself is an eternal exchange of love, Father, Son and Holy Spirit and he has destined us to share in that exchange". (Catechism of the Catholic Church 221).

Westcott wrote, "These three phrases ("God is Spirit, Light, Love") do not simply specify properties of God (as "God is loving") but so far as we can apprehend them, essential attributes of his nature". C.H. Dodd noted that "God is love" means more than "God loves us" and refers to his very nature. De Chardin, after acknowledging the difficulty that many find with the doctrine, wrote "...the Trinitarian nature of God is not a concept which is without any specific relevance for our most immediate religious needs. On the contrary it is manifestly the essential condition of God's inherent capacity to be personal..." (Christianity and Evolution).

We could also approach this from the human side. We are not isolated, self-sufficient individuals. If we are made in the image of God, this reflects, although imperfectly, a "complexity" within God.

Our Lord showed this link between his people's love for each other and his love with the Father before the creation (John 17: 11 & 24).

Many have felt, as Schleiermacher expressed it, that since the doctrine of the Holy Trinity cannot be part of our religious consciousness, it is irrelevant. This hymn expresses the opposite, orthodox view: "God is love" springs from the Holy Trinity and we are drawn into this love. The doctrine therefore lies at the heart of our faith and life.

Epiphany Hymn
For offertory at Holy Eucharist   7777D

Saviour, King and Lord Divine,
Shown forth once in threefold sign,
Frankincense and myrrh and gold,
Wise Men's off'rings brought of old.
Threefold Sign your people still
In our life and work fulfil,
Lay as gifts before your feet,
Lord, whose presence here we greet.

Gold, fit for Christ our King;
Loyal service here we bring,
Goods and homes and honest gain,
Daily work of hands and brain,
Produce of the earth and vine,
Symbolised in bread and wine,
All we offer at your board:
Blest are you, Creator Lord.

Frankincense, the sign of praise:
Lift up hearts and voices raise.
Heav'n and earth your glory fills
Whom we praise with varied skills,
Colour, lights, and organ's tone.
Holy One are you alone.
Angel choirs with ours unite,
God from God and Light from Light.

Myrrh, sad sign of suffering:
Broken, contrite hearts we bring,
Some, their bodies' failing powers,
Mem'ries kept of joyful hours,
Persecuted or afraid,
Hopes forlorn or trust betrayed.
Lamb of God, our sins you bore
Grant us peace, our hearts implore.

Your true presence here we know,
Seen by Wise Men long ago.
Deeper than that outward sign
Is th'indwelling life divine.
Sent in power, our thanks we give,
For your praise to work and live.
Homeward paths the same we trace,
But with hearts transformed by grace.

16

Epiphany Hymn on facing page
This hymn was written for use at the Offertory during the Holy Eucharist. It has been sung to Aberystwyth.

NOTES and MEDITATION from some passages of Holy Scripture and from the Liturgy. There are of course many other passages of Hold Scripture where these themes are found.

Verse 1:   Gospel of St Matthew 2: 1-12 Visit of the Magi
Verse 2:   Romans 12: 1 "Present your bodies as a living sacrifice..."
              Liturgy: "Blessed are You, Lord God of all creation..."
Verse 3:   Isaiah 6:3"Holy, holy, holy..."
              Hebrews 13:15 "Let us offer the sacrifice of praise."
              Liturgy: the Sanctus: God from God (Creed)
Verse 4:   Psalm 51: 17 "The sacrifice of God is a broken spirit: A broken and contrite heart, O God, you will not despise."
              Liturgy: Confession: Penitential Rite: Agnus Dei
Verse 5:   Gospel of St Matthew 2: 12 "They went home by a different way."
              Gospel of St John 6: 56, 14: 22-23 etc.
              Liturgy: The Dismissal: "Go in peace."

The thought is that the Magi met and saw the Lord and went home by a different way. We meet the Lord and instead of seeing him receive his Presence within us. Instead of going home by a different way, we go home as different people, transformed by grace.

Hymn on the Transfiguration 7.7.7.7.7.7. Tune: Ratisbon

Son transformed in light divine
When the Father's voice was heard
From the clouds, a sacred sign
Which proclaimed th'Incarnate Word.
        Give us faith to see your light
        Shining in the darkest night.

Christ, with whom two saints of old,
Seen in glory by your side,
In that glory yet foretold
Suff'rings of the Crucified:
        Help us see and so proclaim
        Glory in the cross of shame.

Saviour, known when we in prayer
Meditate on words sublime,
When your very life we share
Giv'n in transformed Bread and Wine:
        Though we do not see your face
        May we be transformed by grace.

Risen Lord, when we return
To the duller plain below
And our hearts within us burn
For creation seems aglow:
        Help us see with wond'ring eyes
        Transformed nature round us lies.

Lord of life, each plant and tree
Seem transformed by magic word:
Brighter flowers on earth we see
Sweeter sounds the song of bird;
        Brighter visions yet remain:
        Come, Lord Jesus, come and reign.

King of glory. Lord most dear,
Dwelling in our hearts by grace.
When in glory you appear,
Then we shall behold your face.
        So may we your glory share
        And, transformed, your likeness wear.

18

Hymn on the Transfiguration on facing page

Each verse begins with a title of our Lord and finishes with a prayer.
Verse 1: SON. The Father proclaimed Him as "my beloved Son." The
Transfiguration in Synoptic Gospels is a focal point where his divine
nature is revealed. St John shows how the divine continually works
through his human nature.
Verse 2: CHRIST. The Messiah foretold by the Law (Moses) and the
Prophets (Elijah) suffering for us.
Verse 3: SAVIOUR. The One who restores our fallen nature by
grace. The focal points of his continual indwelling are the Scriptures
and the Eucharist.
Verse 4: RISEN LORD. On the Emmaus Road (Luke 24) "our hearts
burned within us." This leads onto –
Verse 6: LORD of LIFE. The Transformation of all nature.
"Magic Word" comes from Eichendorff's romantic vision of nature –
Schläft ein Lied in allen Dingen,
Die da träumen fort und fort:
Und die Welt hebt an zu singen,
Triffst du nur das Zauberwort.
(A song sleeps in everything and the world bursts into song if you
but knew the magic word). Lines 5 and 6 lead on to
Verse 6: KING of GLORY. His Coming "in glory and his kingdom
will have no end." LORD MOST DEAR. Our love for his appearing.
"Christ's glory is promised to all the faithful whom he wishes by his
transformation to enkindle with a desire for that glory." (Aquinas:
Summa 3a. 45.3). Line 5, "Come Lord Jesus" – Revelation 22: 20.
Lines 3 and 4 look back to verse 3, lines 5 and 6. There is throughout
the traditional theology of Nature transformed by Grace leading to
the final Glory.
Holy Scriptures:
Our Lord's Transformation – Matthew 17: 1 - 8, Mark 9: 2-18, Luke
9: 28-38
Glory: Glory of the Cross – John 1: 14, 12: 20-26, 17: 1-4 etc.
The transformed life – 2 Peter 1: 12-21, 2 Corinthians 3: 18
God's glory in nature – Many Psalms
Final transformation – all creations. Revelation 21: 1-4
God's People – 1 John 3: 1-3, 1 Corinthians 15, Philippians 3:21

Mary as a Model of the Church
A Meditative Poem with notes

The Virgin who God's Son once bore
Blessed, unique, will ever be,
Yet in her life for evermore
A model of God's Church we see.

Mary, to whom God's message came,
Confessed no sense of guilt or sin,
Model of sinners cleansed from stain,
By Jesus' blood made pure within.

The Virgin Gabriel's word received,
Though wond'ring how this thing could be,
Model of trust that has believed
God's word in faith, but cannot see.

Chosen God's purpose to fulfil,
She called herself the Lord's handmaid,
Model of firm unshaken will
Obeying though at first afraid.

In Mary's womb alone there grew,
Spirit conceived, the Word made flesh,
Model of all in whom, anew
Of Spirit born, Christ grows afresh.

The Mother's soul, her Saviour's birth
Awaiting, magnified the Lord.
Model of praise the Church on earth
Offers with hymn and sacred word.

Her spirit at this first of joys
With joy abounding overflowed.
Model of joy that none destroys,
By Holy Spirit now bestowed.

The Mother, standing by the Cross,
Would feel her heart pierced by a sword,
Model of sorrows, pain and loss,
The Church must suffer with her Lord.

What joy she felt, her Son to meet,
Found living! (Lost for those three days.)
"Risen indeed!" His people greet
Each other with their Easter praise.

Mary with others came to share
Their vigil till the Spirit came.
Model of Holy Church whose prayer
Still longs for Pentecostal flame.

Our Lady, earthly work now past,
Lives in the Glory of the Lord,
Model of Church, complete at last,
When all creation is restored.

Mary as a Model of the Church
Notes
Much modern thought about Mary sees her as a Model – or Pattern or Symbol – of the Church, and since the Church is made up of individuals, of the individual Christian.

Verse 1. Mary is unique because Jesus is unique, the incarnate Son of the Father. In spite of her uniqueness – or from some aspects, because of it – Mary is also a Model of the Church. Hence Vatican 2 included the section on Mary as part of the section on the Church, of which she is the "model and perfect exemplar in faith and charity."

Verse 2. Exodus 3 and 4, Isaiah 6: 1-9, Jeremiah 1: 6, Luke 5: 8, 1 Timothy 1: 15
Many whom God called responded with reluctance or a sense of unworthiness. Mary's response was without reluctance or sense of unworthiness.
Theological note: After centuries of debate, the dogma of the Immaculate Conception in the Roman Church was promulgated in 1854. The Eastern Church does not accept this, but sees Mary as "all holy" with no actual sin. Other Christians are content to see her as in a specially deep relationship of grace. Since the dogma refers to "in consideration of the merits of Christ Jesus the Saviour of mankind," all Christians see Mary as a model of salvation through Jesus.

Verse 3. Luke 1: 38, John 20: 29
"Blessed are those who have not seen and yet have believed." To believe and accept when the future is uncertain is not sin, but holiness.

Verse 4. Luke 11: 27-28
"Mary is more blessed because she embraces faith Christ then because she conceives the flesh of Christ" (Augustine).

Verse 5. John 1: 13, Galatians 4: 19, Luke 1: 35
Theological note: Origen, writing of the birth of Jesus through the Holy Spirit, wrote of the birth of Jesus in every believer. Aquinas wrote of the threefold birth of Christ. "The first is his eternal birth, which is hidden from us...The Lord said unto me: Thou art my Son, this day I have begotten thee." The second is his nativity in time and the spiritual birth whereby Christ rises as the daystar in our hearts (2 Peter 1: 19). The third is Christ's temporal and bodily birth, as he went forth from the Virgin's womb, becoming visible to us by being clothed in flesh: "Unto us a Son is born," c.f. the Christmas hymn, "Be born in us today." See page 48.

Verse 6. Luke 1: 46-55
The Magnificat, traditionally used to worship. God is glorified in Mary.

Verse 7. Luke 1: 47, John 15: 11, John 16:22, Galatians 5:22 (a different word in Greek)
"Your joy no one will take from you": "The fruit of the Spirit is love, joy..."

Verse 8. Luke 2: 35. A sword shall pierce your own soul also"
John 19: 25. "Standing by the cross of Jesus were his mother..."
Matthew 10: 38. "...take up his cross"
Philippians 3: 10. "...share his sufferings"
and elsewhere
"The sufferings of the Saints are not beneficial to the Church for redemption but for exhortation and example" (Aquinas). See poem "Sacrifice" on page 44.

Verse 9. Luke 3: 41-51. Jesus as a boy was lost for three days. "His Father's business at the end of three days in the Temple was not different from His Father's business at the end of three days in the grave. Like all other incidents in his infancy, this one bore witness to the Mission of the Cross. All men are born to live. He was born to do His Father's business, which was to die and thereby to save. These first recorded words seem like the buds of a passion flower. On Easter Sunday Mary would find Him again in the temple – the temple of His glorified Body." (Fulton J Sheen)

Verse 10. Acts 1: 14

Verse 11
Romans 8:21, Revelation 21, Colossians 1: 19 and elsewhere
"Just as in Mary we see what the Church is in her 'pilgrimage of faith'; so we see what the Church will be in the homeland at the end of her journey." (Catechism) Going back to the verses on the Annunciation – "a kind of spiritual marriage is taking place between the Son of God and human nature. The Virgin's consent, then, which was sought during the course of the Annunciation, stood for the consent of all" (Aquinas), Ephesians 1: 9-10. So we look forward to the final consummation when fully "the dwelling of God will be with men."

The Wounds of Christ
Meditative Verses

These verses start with the words to Thomas in John, chapter 20, verse 26, then continue with thoughts from relevant parts of Scripture and finish with the appearance to Thomas taken up into a fuller vision. To show the progress of thought the final line of each verse is reflected in the first line of the following verse.

"Behold my hands, behold my feet,
And feel my wounded side:"
Know by these scars the Lord you greet
Is Jesus crucified.

The Lord on earth once crucified
Still bears in realms above
Those cruel scars now glorified
As marks of wondrous love:

The marks of love that bore the pain
To set us sinners free:
The Lamb that once in time was slain
Reigns through eternity.

He reigns, whose battle scars proclaim
His victory complete:
The living one, though scars remain
Will never know defeat.

Defeat we often face and loss:
Yet one who knows our need
Still bears the marks of his own cross,
Our great High Priest indeed.

Our great High Priest who intercedes
Before his Father's throne,
The living One who for us pleads
In broken bread is known:

In broken bread and wine outpoured,
Of piercèd flesh the sign,
Within our midst the Risen Lord
The Lamb of God divine:

The Lamb of God whose wounds are strong –
More than his wrath – to keep
Us sinners from a treach'rous wrong
Against a love so deep.

For love so deep – not wrath alone –
Will be the Judge we face,
When th'awful depth of sin is shown
As scorn of costly grace.

That costly grace should be our theme,
His scars our strange delight,
Which inward eye alone has seen,
Still veiled to outward sight.

Unveiled at last we hope to meet
Our Lord once crucified.
"Behold my hands, behold my feet,"
His wounds now glorified.

By transformed wounds of love we'll know
Our Saviour evermore,
And kneel as Thomas long ago,
our Lord and God adore.

The Wounds of Christ
A meditative poem

Passages from Holy Scripture
John 19: 37, 20: 20, 27-28
Luke 24: 30, 36-40
Revelation 1: 7, 5: 6, 6: 16, 13: 8
1 John 2: 1-2
Zechariah 12: 10
Hebrews 2: 18, 4: 14, 7: 25

Two Hymns
Those dear tokens of his passion,
Still his dazzling body bears,
Cause of endless exultation
To his ransomed worshippers:
With what rapture
Gaze we on those glorious scars
                    Lo! He Comes *Charles Wesley*

Crown him the Lord of love!
Behold his hands and side,
Rich wounds yet visible above
In beauty glorified:
No angel in the sky
Can fully bear that sight,
But downward bends his burning eye
At mysteries so bright.
                    Crown him *M Bridges*

Artwork
Some crosses and crucifixes are simple and rough, to express the reality
of the Crucifixion and of suffering; some are splendid and costly, to
express the beauty of love. Some representations of the Last Judgement
show Christ displaying the wounds of the Passion.

Mystical Writing
An example is St Bernard on the Song of Songs, chapter 2, verse 14:
"Someone has interpreted the "clefts of the rock" as meaning the
Wounds of Christ, and fitly too for Christ is the Rock. Blessed are the
clefts which proved to Thomas that Christ was risen and that He was
God!..., where indeed are there complete security and rest for us frail
men, save in the Saviour's wounds?..."

The Wounds of Christ
Theological Exegesis
St Thomas Aquinas, Summa 3a 54: 4

On the other hand the Lord said to Thomas, Put your finger here; look here are my hands. Give me your hand; put it into my side.

It was fitting that in the resurrection Christ's soul take up once more a body with wounds. This was so first of all for the sake of his own glory, for Bede tells us that he preserved his wounds not from any inability to cure them, but that there might be a perpetual sign of his glorious triumph. Augustine continues this line of reasoning. Perhaps in the kingdom of God we shall see on the bodies of the martyrs marks of those wounds which they received for the sake of Christ's name; in their bodies this will not be a sign of deformity but of dignity. From these wounds, though they are in the body, will shine forth a beauty which is not from the body but is the result of virtue.

Secondly, these wounds are ordered to strengthen the hearts of the disciples in their belief in Christ's resurrection.

Thirdly, so that during Christ's prayer to his Father for us he might manifest constantly the type of death he bore for the sake of mankind.

Fourthly, so that by placing before their eyes the very marks of death he might show those whom he redeemed by this death how mercifully he came to their aid.

Finally, to show on judgement day how just the condemnation will be. As Augustine remarks, Christ knew why he kept the scars on his body. He showed them to Thomas who did not believe until he touched and saw them. So too will he show them to his enemies to convince them by his proclamation of Truth itself: Look at the man whom you have crucified. You see the wounds you have inflicted. You recognise the side which you have pierced: it was opened by you for your own benefit, yet you did not wish to enter therein.

Hence: 1. These wounds which remained in Christ's body are not wounds of corruption or of defect. Since they are signs of virtue, they are ordered to manifest a greater degree of glory. There even appeared in the places where the wounds were a special type of beauty.

27

The Church as Bride of Christ
A Meditative Poem

Eternal God, whose love o'erflowed
To create our human race,
With all natural gifts bestowed
Union with Himself by grace.

For union in our human life
To reflect His love divine,
He made the love of man and wife
Of His love the mystic sign.

Though human sin this love betrayed,
God was ever faithful shown.
A Nuptial Covenant was made
With the folk He called His own.

This Covenant was made of old,
Which a newer would fulfil.
In prophetic word foretold
Was a union deeper still.

Our Lord to make this union came.
With the Father ever one,
He took our fully human frame,
Lived on earth th'eternal Son

The Son, Whose arms reached out to save,
On the cross were opened wide,
His fully human life He gave
To embrace the Church His Bride.

Christ and the Holy Church His Bride
Now are one in union deep,
While each soul for whom he died
Christ will in communion keep.

This deep communion of the Bride
Will in deeper way be known,
When Christ, the Lamb once crucified,
Leads her to her heav'nly home.

In the heavenly home at last
At the lamb's great wedding day
Evil and sin and tears are past:
Joy and gladness ever stay.

In the joy there celebrated
Are prophetic words fulfilled.
Heaven and earth anew created
Know the union God had willed.

That union each invited guest
Finds in Eucharist foretold,
When we come, unworthy, blest,
And the lamb of God behold.

Notes of The Church as Bride of Christ

"This is a great mystery and I take it to mean Christ and the Church."
Ephesians 5: 21-32
Gospels – Mark 10: 2-9

In this passage St Paul writes about three relationships – husband / wife, children / parents and master / slaves. Aristotle also wrote about these three relationships, but concentrated more on the master / slave relationship and the theory of slavery. (Politics 1:3). Philo gave an allegorical interpretation to Genesis 2:24 as referring to Mind, Sense, Perception etc (Legum Allegoriae 2:49). In a less obscure way he also referred it to husband / wife (Quaestiones 1:29).

Of the three relationships the Apostle deals most fully with husband / wife. He interprets Genesis 2:24 as referring primarily to Christ and the Church. If, in these politically correct days, some are unhappy about the language of authority and obedience, it should be realised that this is in a context of love, different from the master / servant relationship. This means that marriage is not just a human institution useful for illustrating our relationship with God, but that our relationship with God is primary and marriage reflects this. On the negative side, an offence against matrimony is an offence against the heart of the Christian faith. It is therefore appropriate that this is part of the Epistle whose theme is our final destiny in Christ, as shown in the opening passage.

Old Testament. Examples:
Genesis – Creation of man and woman in image of God for fellowship with God.
Jeremiah 2:2   Ezekiel 16 etc
Hosea 1 etc   Psalm 45
Song of Solomon: Interpreted as referring to the relationship between Israel and YHWH and then between Christ and the Church.

New Testament. Examples:
2 Corinthians 11:2   Ephesians 5
Revelation 19:6-10; 21:2,9

Themes and close union, sacrificial self-giving and the converse – unfaithfulness.

"Sacred scripture begins with the creation of man and woman in the image and likeness of God and concludes with a vision of "the wedding feast of the Lamb." Scripture speaks throughout of marriage and its "mystery", its institution and the meaning God has given it, its origin and its end, its various realisations throughout the history of salvation, the difficulties arising from sin and its renewal "in the Lord", i.e. the New Covenant of Christ and the Church."

"The nuptial covenant between God and his people Israel had prepared the way for the new and everlasting covenant in which the Son of God, by becoming incarnate and giving his life, has united to himself in a certain way all mankind saved by him, thus preparing for "the wedding feast of the Lamb" (Catechism of the Catholic Church 1602, 1612).

The Preface to the Marriage Service in the Anglican Service Books-
"Holy matrimony is an honourable estate, instituted of God in the time of man's innocency, signifying unto us the mystical union that is betwixt Christ and his church." (Book of Common Prayer).

"Marriage is a gift of God in creation... they shall be united with one another in heart, body and mind, as Christ is united with his bride the Church." (Common Worship).

Both of these statements are in keeping with the teaching of Aquinas-

"Marriage was instituted in the state of innocence not by virtue of being a sacrament, but in the virtue of being "in oficium naturae". Nevertheless, because of what it was going to become it signified a future reality concerning Christ and the church, just as all other things served as prefiguring Christ." (Summa 3a.61.2)

In other words, while marriage is part of natural law, it is raised to sacramental status as an expression of Christ and his church. This is sometimes expressed in corporate, sometimes in individual, terms-

St Bernard on the Church and individual
"...you must understand by them (the Lovers) not a man and a woman, but the Word and the Soul. And if I say "Christ and the Church" instead of Word and Soul, the difference is only this: that by the Church is meant the unity – or rather unanimity of many souls." (Song of Songs LXI: 2)

In this depth of personal union we may place the "Mystical Marriage" of St Catherine of Siena and the references in St Thérèse, for example, to mon Époux.

We come back to Ephesians 5: What is, for all, the heart of our faith is our union with our Lord Jesus Christ.

31

Notes on the three following hymns

Easter Gifts
This is based on St John's Gospel, chapter 20, verses 19-31, one of the Gospel readings for the Easter season.
Joy – "The disciples were glad when they saw the Lord."
Peace – "Peace be with you." (Expressed in the sharing of Peace at the Eucharist).
Grace – "Whose sins you forgive they are forgiven." (Absolution at Eucharist).
Last verse – "As the Father has sent me, so I send you." (Dismissal at Eucharist).
Written with the tune Bewdley in mind, but this is not well known. It has usually been sung to Palms of Glory and to Monkland.

Garden Hymn
This was first written for, and first sung at, a visit to a garden with church members from the German city of Freiburg, twinned with Guildford. The theme of peace and healing of the nations therefore had a special significance. The hymn uses garden scenes to express the Christian Faith, God's good Creation and the Fall, where supernatural grace was lost and the image of God marred, but not completely lost, our Lord's sacrifice and Resurrection, giving new life to us, and the final Resurrection, visualised in the Book of Revelation. There is a contrast between verses 3 and 5 – "slyly" and "sadly", calling "Adam" and "Mary" by name. The tune is Bread of Heaven.

Church Bells
An attempt is made here to express both the joys and solemnity of the Faith through the rhythm.

Easter Gifts
Based on John 20:19-31

Easter gifts this day our King,
Risen from the grave, will bring:
As of old he comes to greet
His disciples when we meet.

Gift of joy makes glad the heart,
Joy that never need depart.
"Alleluia!" Voices raise:
"Christ is risen!" joyful praise.

Gift of peace that calms and cheers
In a world of hates and fears.
We receive his peace divine:
Share together word and sign.

Gift of grace that comes to bless
Those who sin and guilt confess.
Through his priests there still is heard
Jesus' own forgiving word.

Gift of joy and gift of peace,
Gift of pardon and release.
Christ who died and rose we know:
Broken bread his wounds now show.

Christ, once by the Father sent,
Sends us from his sacrament,
In his world to show "He lives!"
Joy and peace through us he gives.

Garden Hymn

In a Garden long ago,
In a far-off Paradise,
God gave life that plants may grow,
Birds that sing in peaceful skies.
God the Lord rejoiced to bless
His created loveliness.

In the Garden then so fair,
God gave to our human race
Image of himself to share,
Aided by supernal grace,
Gave to till the fruitful ground,
One with nature all around.

To that Garden Satan came,
Slyly tempted man and wife.
Adam hid when called by name,
Left us sin and death and strife.
God's grace lost, his image marred,
Nature now seemed harsh and hard.

In a garden Jesus knelt,
Drank the cup of bitter pain:
In his sinless soul he felt
All our sin and guilt and shame:
Garden of Gethsemane,
Scene of Jesus' agony.

To a Garden Mary came
Sadly to anoint the dead:
Heard a voice that called her name,
Met the Lord of Life instead:
Garden of the risen Lord,
Paradise is here restored.

In a Garden, dream-revealed,
Crystal water, tree of life,
By whose leaves are nations healed:
No more sin or death or strife.
Garden of Immanuel,
God at last with us will dwell.

Hymn on Church Bells

8.7.8.7.8.7.8.7.   Possible tune: Golden Sheaves – NEH 261

Church bells resound the world around
From lofty tower and steeple.
Their ringing's heard like spoken word,
To summon all the people.
On holy days, come, come to praise,
Come join in prayer together.
Their sound from high tells passers-by
God lives, God reigns for ever.

Church bells rejoice with happy voice
Where happy folk are meeting:
On festal days, come, come and raise
Your notes with welcome greeting.
At wedding times your joyful chimes
Proclaim a happy ending:
The church bells ring, the people sing,
Their notes together blending.

Deep sounds one bell to toll the knell:
One soul in death has slumbered:
To those who mourn, it seems to warn
Our years of life are numbered.
Yet deep notes teach God cares for each
And takes us in his keeping.
Steady its beat, its measured feet
Gives hopes of peaceful sleeping.

Church bells resound the world around:
Give God, give God the glory.
The air they fill: our hearts they thrill:
Come hear the Christian story.
Skilled hands employ, creating joy,
Their many changes weaving,
Or solemn tone when one alone
Tells that one soul is leaving.

We too proclaim our saviour's name,
Our heart with voice uniting:
Tell out, tell out with joyful shout,
All other folk inviting.
Some lack belief, some sunk in grief:
All hear that God is living.
Our lips declare, as faith we share,
The joy our God is giving.

A short meditation on St Luke's Gospel 10:17-20

Jesus said, "Do not rejoice in this, that the evil spirits are subject to you, but rejoice that your names are written in heaven."

Lord Jesus, at this evening hour
We turn with joy to thee
In devils subject to thy power
And captive souls set free.

Yet while our eager hearts confide
The tale of victories won.
Guard us from joy that turns to pride
On hearing thy, "Well done."

Lest while rejoicing we should make
These victories our plea
Grant us as penitents to take
Our place at Calvary

There kneeling make our only plea
Thy cross, and hear thy voice:
"In heaven your names are known to me:
Only in this rejoice."

St John of the Cross, in a long passage on rejoicing in good works, speaks of the dangers which may accompany this, such as pride and presumption, and expounds this passage from Luke 10—

Our Lord rebuked his disciples when they returned to Him with joy because they had power over evil spirits, saying: Rejoice not in this, that spirits are subject to you, but rejoice in this, that your names are written in heaven. This means in the book of life. Man therefore ought not to rejoice unless he is walking in the right way, doing his works in charity. Now that love cannot be perfect if it is not strong enough to purify itself from all joy in these things and to find it only in doing the will of God. (The Ascent of Carmel III. 27-30).

Referring to a particular sign of the letter T, Ste Thérèsa of Lisieux wrote —

Astre divin, O sagesse profonde
Vous répandez vos ineffable dons
Sur les petits, les pauvres de ce monde
Et dans le ciel vous écrivez leurs noms.

St Mary Magdalene. A Meditative Poem

The first grey streaks of heavenly dawn
That break upon earth's gloom
Show Mary weeping, lone, forlorn.
Her heart with bitter anguish torn
Beside an empty tomb.

Once she had knelt by Jesus' side
With penitential tear,
Kissing the feet her hair had dried,
Wept with relief when flung aside
Lay all her guilty fear.

The ointment poured upon his feet
Scented the evening air,
And life seemed but a fragrance sweet
Where all the joys of heaven meet
To banish earthly care.

A flower-strewn path for her to tread
Lit by eternal day,
Faithful she stepped where Jesus led.
But fading drooped the flowers ahead
And darker grew the way.

Onward he strode: she followed still
Not straying from his side,
Until at last, midst mocking shrill
And jeering crowds on Calvary's hill
She saw him crucified,

And all seemed lost. This moment brief
Is left her to display
With ointment poured her bitter grief –
Sad echo of a lost belief
And distant, happier day.

Yet now there waits a deeper pain,
For standing there apart
She sees her final act is vain
Empty the place where he had lain
And emptier Mary's heart.

And Mary's tears so free to flow
Are blinding Mary's sight.
Alone she bears her deepest woe.
Adoring heart, how bright that glow!
Oh soul, how dark this night!

Those tears from penitence for sin
Are sweet, for though they mar
Awhile the face, they cannot dim
The spark of hope that deep within
Gleams like a sudden star.

But when the vision fades and flee
The last sad sparks of hope,
When we who walked so far with thee
Finding our eyes no longer see
In empty darkness grope.

Backward our wistful glance we cast
On faith's first vivid gleams.
Doubts and despair for ever past.
We thought those joys were meant to last
Not fade as empty dreams.

And while our mourning glance we turn
On feelings that have died,
While for the past our hearts still yearn,
Blinded, our eyes cannot discern
The Saviour by our side.

Our vision, feeble yet must grow,
And growing oft brings pain.
Though once familiar thoughts may go,
Yet still our Saviour's voice we know
That softly calls our name.

At Jesus' call she lifts her head,
Then calm all inward strife.
Her sorrows with the darkness fled,
No more she seeks among the dead
The risen Lord of life.

On our soul's night there shines again
Thy face, but in a blaze
Of cleaner light, thy love the same
Shows that the tomb dare nothing claim
But our too narrowed gaze.

Notes for Meditation on St Mary Magdalene

This poem follows the tradition, often expressed in paintings and glass, of identifying Mary Magdalene, out of whom Jesus cast seven devils (Luke 8:2) with the woman "who was a sinner" (Luke 7:37) and with Mary, the sister of Martha (John 12:3). Both anointed Jesus. The Gospels do not state this identification. In her play, "The Man born to be King," Dorothy Sayers did so, to make a "tie-rod" for individual episodes, pointing out that St Augustine and Pope Gregory the Great had done so. The thoughts for our spiritual life in general are not dependent on this particular identification, although this poem uses it as material for meditation.

Joy is shown by the words of our Lord and throughout the Scriptures to be God's gift to us, and is therefore a mark of the spiritual life. Our Lord, however, warned us in the Parable of the Sower of those, "who receive the word with joy," but having no root fall away when trouble comes.

In keeping with this, many spiritual teachers warn us that excessive feelings of joy and devotion at the beginning may not last. St John of the Cross wrote, "Many beginners, delighting in the sweetness and joy of their spiritual occupations, strive after spiritual sweetness, rather than purity and discretion.....They who are bent on spiritual sweetness, labour also under another very great imperfection: excessive weakness and remissness on the rugged road of the cross, for the soul that is given to sweetness naturally sets itself against all the pain of self-denial." (Dark Night of the Soul" Book 1, Chapter 6).

John Newton described the spiritual life as not like Jonah's gourd, which quickly sprung up and quickly withered, but like an acorn which grows steadily into an oak.

"When I see any, soon after they appear to be awakened, making a speedy profession of great joy before they have a due acquaintance with their own hearts, I am in pain for them..." (Letter of September. 3rd 1776)

In these two quotations we see an example of affinity between Catholic and Evangelical spirituality.

Most people's spiritual lives have "Ups and Downs," and it would be an exaggeration to equate every "Down" with St John's "Dark Night of the Soul." The church's spiritual writers give us both warning and encouragement, and with this aim this meditative poem is offered.

Gethsemane

Our Saviour in Gethsemane,
Piercing with patient eye
The gath'ring gloom, what did he see
That caused his agony?

Before his searching gaze appears
Our long sad tale of woe,
Mankind with all its guilt and fears
That only he can know.

Each life befouled by inborn stain,
Where loathsome thoughts have grown
To loveless words and deeds of shame
He sees and makes his own.

Yet while he mourns to see our Fall
From what we might have been.
Could he see beyond it all,
Beyond this present scene?

Before God's throne in spotless white
They stand, all tears are dried,
And in a blaze on endless light
They praise the Lamb who died.

The gath'ring gloom for ever past
When daylight dawns again,
And did he, seeing this at last,
Feel joy within his pain?

Gethsemane: Notes

We stand, or rather kneel, on holy ground, as we meditate in this little poem on the Saviour bearing the sin and suffering of the world. Two passages on Gethsemane may help us to enter into this.

The first attributed to John Tauler (1300-1361). "Now of a truth, Christ took all the sins of the world upon himself, and of his own will he allowed sorrow of heart for these sins to come upon him, even as if he himself had committed them. And because of his divine wisdom which saw all things, he beheld all sins, especially those that were most hateful, that ever have been or ever will be: and at the same time he beheld the contempt and wrong which they inflicted on his Father".

The second is from Newman's, "The Mental Sufferings of our Lord in his Passion". "What was it he had to bear, when He thus opened upon His soul the torment of this predestined pain? He had to bear the weight of sin: He had to bear the weight of your sin: He had to bear the sins of the whole world..... They are upon Him, they are all but His own, for He is the one Victim for us all, the Sole Satisfaction, the real Penitent, all but the real sinner".

Devotion must be based on sound theology: emotion and intellect together. For our spiritual life Christ bore the sins of each because he bore the sins of all. His sufferings in time as man have this infinite value because He is the eternal Son. "This pain of Christ surpassed any pain ever felt by a penitent, first because it proceeded from a greater wisdom and love, by which the pain of contrition is increased, and second, because He suffered for all sins at once (pro omnibus peccatis simul doluit). As Isaiah said Truly it was our infirmities he bore". (Aquinas Summa 3a.46.6)

The passage from Isaiah 53 on the Suffering Servant, quoted by Aquinas, finishes on a note of triumph at the salvation accomplished. "Jesus, for the joy set before him, endured the cross." (Hebrews 12:2). So this poem finishes on this note of joy.

Sacrifice

Our Saviour, who alone did take
The bitter cup his Father gave,
Offered his perfect life to make
One sacrifice his world to save.

His blood upon the cross once shed
Imparts his life through cup of wine,
Whereby our thirsting souls are fed,
Abiding in the one true vine.

His body, offered in our stead,
All signs and symbols did fulfil
His mystic body, with the Head,
Is offered now to do his will.

So while in sacred rite we claim
The benefit his passion won,
We also share his cup of pain
And make his sacrifice our own.

Ourselves upon the altar laid,
Each sinful deed his death must share:
Body and soul all offering made
Must make his will their only care.

Imperfect now, complete at last,
In Christ, his Kingdom fully come.
Creation, history, present, past
Will all be offered up as one.

The first poems dealt with memory, past experiences becoming part of us, living in "Proustian" images, something of our general human experience. These final poems now look at the theme from a deeper and specifically Christian viewpoint.

"Gethsemane" meditates on the eternal Son, mystically united with the human race, bearing the sins of the whole world in his human flesh. "Sacrifice" expresses two truths. Firstly, our Lord's sacrifice is unique, the perfect act of homage, fulfilling all symbols and making complete atonement for sin. Secondly, he calls his people to take up their cross (e.g. Matthew 16:24) and the Epistles speak of sharing his sufferings as well as his resurrection (e.g. Philippians 3:10, Colossians 1:24 and 1 Peter 4:13). Aquinas made clear a truth always stressed by Evangelicals, that only Christ's sufferings are for redemption –

"The sufferings of the saints are not beneficial to the Church by way of redemption, but of encouragement and example (2 Corinthians 1:6)"
(Summa 3a. 48:5)

"Sharing Christ's sufferings" suggests the past experience of Christ becoming part of the present life of his people. [See the poem "The Wounds of Christ" – the eternally glorified Lord bears the marks of his passion]. This is bound up with fulfilling our destiny – union with Christ through love. While this involves the whole life, it is sacramentally expressed in the Holy Eucharist, where we receive the fruit of the one Sacrifice – union with Christ – and offer ourselves with him.

"We are the body of Christ...in the oblation the church is offered."
(Augustine. City of God 10:6)

The centre of Christian worship, the Holy Eucharist, is not simply a mental recollection of a past event. It is a "making present" of the One Sacrifice. Recent study has emphasised the "memorial" in the Passover as full of the reality of the events which it commemorates. The Eucharist unites past, present – but also the future. After writing of redemption through the cross, the Apostle presents us with God's purpose – "to gather up all things in Christ, things in heaven and things on earth." Knox translates this "to give history its fulfilment by resuming everything in him." (Ephesians 1:10).

The poem on the facing page take up this thought, inspired by a later verse in the same Epistle (Ephesians 4:5). A Trinitarian exposition, although not usually regarded as its direct meaning, seemed appropriate here. de Chardin was clear that our starting point is the "Man Jesus recognised and worshipped as God" and that we must hold to the historic character of Christ (that is, the divinity of the historic Christ.) "Based on this, his thoughts reached out to the cosmic Christ and vision of the future, sometimes difficult to understand. The last words in the diary were 'St Paul, the three verses God all in all'."

In Christ, past, present, future, time and eternity come together. As with all of our life in Christ, these have a special focus in the Holy Eucharist.

"As often as you eat this bread and drink this cup, you proclaim the Lord's death until he comes." (1 Corinthians 11:26)

"The Sacrament signifies three things. It looks back to the past: in this it commemorates the passion of the Lord, which was the true sacrifice... with regard to the present, we are united with Christ and with one another... it has a third significance with regard to the future: it foretells that enjoyment of God which will be ours in heaven". (Aquinas Summa 3a. 73. 4)

This theme of the future is present in other poems: the TRANSFIGURATION, with the final Beatific vision, the bereavement Sonnets, with the promise of a reunion with those whom we love.

So this little book which began with a human note of memory and nostalgia finishes with a note of Christian optimism. The God of past, present and future will "gather up all things in Christ."

46

Poem for the New Year

Based on Ephesians 4:5 "God above all, through all, in (you) all.

Lord of all time, your name we
praise,
Living Father, Spirit, Son,
Within whose hand lie long-
past days,
Everlasting Three in One.
For countless gifts of untold
worth,
Thankfully your name we bless:
Our share of sins that spoil
your earth,
Penitent, we now confess.

Lord above all, your name we
praise,
Father, universal source,
Yourself beyond both time and
space,
Maker and life-giving force.
As passing centuries have
rolled
Eager minds your works
explore:
Fresh vistas to our gaze unfold:
Mortals wonder and adore.

Lord through all things your
name we praise,
Son through whom mankind
draws breath,
The Word revealing truth and
grace,

In our nature rose from death.
Your sacrifice in time complete
Will eternal grace retain,
We kneel in love before your
feet,
Yesterday, to-day, the same.

Lord in us all, your name we
praise,
Spirit of prophetic fire,
Through varied ages of our
race,
Human spirits you inspire –
Creative thought and music's
sound,
Colour, light, in works of art,
Yet in a union more profound
Dwell in each believer's heart.

Lord of all time, your name we
praise,
Living Father, Spirit, Son,
Within whose hand lie future
days,
Everlasting Three in One.
Still proceeds our human story
On the varied paths begun,
Till your Kingdom comes in
glory,
Gathering all at last in one.

The Three Births of Christ

Begotten 'ere creation's dawn,
God the Father's only Son.
In th'eternal world is born
With the Father ever one.
In the heavenly realm his dwelling
Unrevealed to human sight,
Mystery beyond all telling.
God from God and Light from Light.

At Bethlehem his human birth,
In our world of time and space,
As Mary's Son he lived on earth,
Giving life and truth and grace,
Whom hands have touched and ears have heard,
Once revealed to human sight.
In darkness shone th'eternal Word
With an uncreated light.

The Word made flesh once more is born
In the soul which him receives,
The daystar rises like the dawn
Shining where the heart believes.
Not of flesh or human will,
Of God's Spirit is this birth,
The Son, whose home is heaven still,
Dwells within his church on earth.

Passages from Holy Scripture
St John's Gospel 1:1-18; 3:1-15; 1 John 1: 1-4; 2 Peter 1:19

Aquinas wrote of the threefold birth of Christ, linking these with three Masses on Christmas Day. (Summa 3a.83.2). See also page 23. He referred to the "daystar rising in our hearts."

Iranaeus wrote of the two births, in eternity and of the Virgin. So in Christ the temporal and human are united with the eternal and divine. (adv, Haer. 3 esp. 19)

This is the heart of our restoration in Christ, by which the temporal and changing are at last taken up into the eternal and unchanging.

Previous Publications by the same author

Unity, Uniformity and the English Church
A R Mowbray 1961

The Second Advent
A R Mowbray 1963

Hymns and Meditations on the Seven Words from the Cross
Searchline Publishing 1999

It's a Cat's Life
Searchline Publishing 2009